BRING AN EXTRY MULE

BRING AN EXTRY MULE

poems

Ken Hada

2017 © Ken Hada
ISBN: 978-0-944048-77-1
purple flag press / vacpoetry.org
Design by Regina Schroeder
Cover Photo by Steven Schroeder
Acknowledgements follow text.

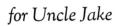

for Uncle Jake

Prologue: Bring an Extry Mule

As If Life Is Just A Song

Sunflowers Rising Yellow
Primal & Proud

Like Vagrant Birds Fluttering Above A Fencerow

Blades of Conformity

Prologue:
Bring an Extry Mule

If you find yourself
traveling,
the road more than metaphor
the burden not as light
as sometimes advertised,
bear up then
pack your cares
forge the stream
climb the next summit
one foot in front of the other
one piece of truth at a time
flicking away like fish scales.

We'll camp this side
of Jordan
and there we'll sing
the blues until happiness comes
and there know
what peace may be found
as we wait together
for who knows what.

As if Life is Just a Song

The Hard Luck of Not Dying Young

Even those tough, whiskeyslurping
jerkyeating
muleskinned
cactusfaced
sowmouthed
rockballed
bloodysouled
outlawing
gunslinging
bulletbiting
marauding
mutilating
scalping
injunhating
badass
posseridinghombres

at darkest night
under a rustler's moon
in deepest sleep

lay their guilty, sweetlittlejesus face
upon a saddlepillow
holding themselves tender
tucked with a cowboyblankie
curled
in the position neither mothers
nor angels could resist
nor could any fellow rider—
at least for a moment—despise.

Somewhere

1.

beyond the stars
ancestors laugh at our silly dilemmas
and again say litanies to us
we all should know by now
ugly echoes
in the back of our mind

2.

gun shows and dysfunctional families
how much confusion
can we tolerate?
too much talk
too much Jesus talk
gray skies, graying beards, gray hearts
there's nothing to celebrate

3.

you want to tap into a cosmos
you want to feel family
so you be the big brother
and put out endless fires
some which you sparked
trying to be a brother
a son, uncle, dad
you are light cracking
from an ancient cave
laid at the feet of hillbillies
circling campfires
a millennium away
orphaned gypsies forever
coming and going on roads

that bleed both ways
always going somewhere
you don't belong
returning from someplace
you can never know

4.

like tin-can music straining
through a pawn-shop amp
half sounds slapping
a three chord melody
playing church in store fronts
4/4 time—hopeful hands
clapping somewhat in time
throaty praise bumping
the acoustic tiles above
saturated with smoke and water stains
enduring until redemption returns
football on the television
guitar heroes, junk food
and a wal-mart shopping spree

I would like to Say
"pretence accomplishes nothing"
—Seneca

I would like to say that I have returned
from isolation in the moody, desolate
wilderness with a burning tongue—
a message that will right the wrongs,
redeem the times, set captives free,
bring peace to the masses, satisfaction
to my own desires—

           I would like to say
something courageous, virtuous—

              I would like
to connect our contemporary blindness,
our current vitriolic meandering
to our forefathers and mothers who
also endured weird political alliances,
religious zealotry, economic disaster
and bloody war—

           but to link
ourselves so easily to those hardy folks
seems pretentious and pretense
is exactly our problem—

          the delusion
may prove feeble when the full history
of our pathos is finally realized, but it is
our delusion. And we love it, don't we?
We lay on couches bloating ourselves
with casual death, blaming everything
and everyone but ourselves—

                                    while
the desert calls, wilderness hovers
just beyond self-imposed limits,
our safe corridor where we congratulate
ourselves for conforming to nonsense,
pat ourselves on the back for being
obvious, oblivious—
                    but somewhere
out there in the shadows, strange
and forlorn birds mock our noise,
and on the mountain, the ghost
of democracy drifts, a tenuous mist
covering the peaks, the strong,
righteous earth, eternally bound,
so high above our ambition.

Mother's Day: A White Professor Reflects

Their few first days of college
after a football game, the recruits
were invited to a team party
on the Canadian River's white

sandy shores. I never met the mother
of the one murdered that night
by a racist trying to own a river.

I heard the testimony of another
after her son was confined
to a wheelchair for life.
Her graciousness confounds me!

The best friend of the murder victim
was in my class; he witnessed
that night. In an essay, he quoted

some of the last words his friend spoke:
Man look at those stars;
We don't see stars like that back home.

Will water lapping the riverbank
expunge that bloody night?
It will take a lot of water.
Those same stars hang above us all.

Young Mother on a Train

Lemon-green top, black stretch
pants tight around her waist
and legs, stars tattooed on her flesh
bare feet sandaled in braided tan

finally she is allowed to fall asleep
though one ear listens for any missteps
of her two restless boys riding
in the seat in front of her. For now

her arms are folded on her lap
stylish sunglasses hang at her bra-line
a denim jacket draped around her
holds her like she had always dreamed.

On the Death of Lorca

When I think of Lorca's death,
his young life erased
so soon, so unceremoniously

I wonder what is the hope
of poetry, the purpose of words,
why we sing only to die.

*The metaphors live on after
a poet's bones are in the ground*
writes a sympathetic scholar.*

So Lorca lives on despite
attempts to claim and disclaim
responsibility—to make

the poet something he never
was and nothing that we
should fear or admire—just

a life, but some poets seem fated
to live on despite the terror
of the right—their antigay

hatred, their misuse of the poor,
exploitation of resources,
the propagandizing of art.

So Lorca, whose grave is unknown,
whose body is scattered
in the Granada hillside belongs

to us all who wish for justice
and peaceful coexistence.
Art for art's sake, the young poet

mocks, *is something that would be
cruel if it weren't so ridiculous.*
Such is only a fantasy

of the self-indulgent
whose petty revisions of history
insult the memory

of the brave common folk
who resisted Fascism in all its forms
and convenient alliances—

the church and nobility—betrays
those who died because they chose
to think, and in their thinking

chose to be what their oppressors
could never be, could never acquire
by politics, or murder.

Blessed are the poor
and blessed is the man of words
un-swayed by fame or power,

the poet who sees that life and death
are always organic, blended
forever in the soil beneath our feet.

Under a suspicious moon Gypsies
still sing, peasants eat together.
A hard life is no match

for their souls. Lorca was one
of us. Remember his body
and remember his blood.

Even today, his ballads correct
those who appropriate art
to justify their bloody cause.

The murdered poet redeems
all the nameless victims of tyranny,
inspires survivors to think

and write, as long as the right allows,
as long as breath gives birth to hope
and the hopeful gather under clear, dark moons.

*I am quoting Gary Brower, and much of the information suggested
in this poem is gained from his article "Lorca & Neruda: Poetic
Immortality, Political Exhumation." Malpais Review Vol. 4, no. 1,
Summer 2013, 175 – 207.

For This Time, at Least

As darkness descends, this time
in-between, when stars are not yet lit,
the moon lingering far away, I sit
as still as I can, hear whippoorwills,
some in woods just north of me, some
to the south, and for the moment,
look up into soft sky, feel how good
it is to be on this planet, on this piece
of earth, this place in Oklahoma,
and for this time, at least I will not
allow thoughts of a greedy governor
or a corrupt congress—betrayers
of the commonwealth, of common
sense—an emaciated education,
eviscerated common good enter me.

For these moments I will quietly sit
and practice the old art of *wu wei*,
let night birds fill me. I have become
acquainted with the night, ducking
from too much light, a squinting fool
seeking guidance from stealthy birds.
Their song merges with geese honking
high overhead, bark of a distant dog,
cattle lowing, tree frogs tremoring,
cicadas, crickets. I see bats darting
in their nightly duty and am comforted.
For this time, at least I am nothing
but an empty cup waiting to be full again.

Testimony

She sells bait.
She makes biscuits.
She chats up fishermen.
She remembers Odessa
where she danced guilty
before her broken heart
expecting Jesus to return
any moment.

That was the 70's. She still
expects him—*the signs
are everywhere—look
what's goin on down there in Syria.
It's all in the bible.*

What do you think about all that?

Her sweet cloudy eyes,
her wrinkled nose
wait for my answer.

I love her biscuits.
I want to fish.
I tell her she's got it figured out
But I feel bad the way I say it.

She knows I'm lost
but she has borne witness
to her blessed hope.

I leave her trailer.
I hope the fish are biting.
I hope Jesus comes again.
I hope she can forgive herself
for those days in Odessa.

As for me, I think she
must have been beautiful dancing
with a cowboy turned oilman
who left her to survive
selling minnows, making biscuits
for sinners like me.

It only takes a little leaven
to leaven the whole lump.

For her, I will stand quietly
while she testifies.
She has been rescued—sort of.
Like a beaten pup, some creatures
never fully recover. They trust
only what they can touch—
biscuit dough, or minnows
panicked in a tank.

She places the net into the water,
cuts a swath. Some are destined
to be caught. Some escape
this time. Some move from tank
to bucket to hook.

I would believe too if only
I could escape the net.

Maybe I should hang up my rod,
drive to Odessa, lay hands
on some drunk roughneck, or
maybe I should let her pray
for me, or maybe I should leave
her alone.

Until I can make up my mind
there is a lake full of fish—
and biscuits are something
like the bread of life—especially
when she covers them
with black raspberry jam.

Late Night Witness

In the middle of nowhere
in one of those towns hoping to be
what it is not, halfway between midnight
and morning's first light,
I stop in a vacant parking lot
next to a dimly lit gas station
to stretch my legs, rub sleep from my eyes.

I hear the word "faggot"—
I hear a fist popping on flesh, on a jaw—
I look up to see a teen-age boy
with his bike, trying to get to the air pump,
being beaten by a much larger bully
calling him "fag" while another guy
and girl sit smoking.

I see the victim lower his head
trying to resist the blows
while making his way to the air pump—
and then, it is over as quickly as it started.
He gets on his bike and speeds away.

In those ugly seconds, I thought they
would all be gone by the time
I could get the police directed to a place
I hardly knew.

As I moved forward, thinking of interfering,
I thought the big kid would surely whip my ass
before fleeing, and even if I could get the police
interested in finding them, if they could find them,
it would be their three words against mine.

So I'm standing in a starless night thinking
of calling the cops, thinking of approaching them

when the victim suddenly flees in furious, frantic humiliation.
Who knows what the darkness knows?

I tried to imagine the future
for both the bully and the victim
but it only made the night darker.

Disquieting

At the street fair
sweaty beer bottles gripped
with delusion
we hear his words
too cinematic to believe
it could happen in real life

but his turned-down face
downcast, teary eyes

confirm our collective sorrow
for him, sure, but especially for her,
for someone named Elaina
whose brown skin
and dark eyes

may never smile again
captured forever
by the cartel
for whom she dances
for her life.

No romantic tourist
can afford to buy her freedom.
No regular Romeo dare fuck
with Mexican drug lords

so we stand together
on a busy street in Oklahoma City
dumfounded by his story
stupefied in our impotence
our common male desire—cut off.

His voice chokes, quiets,
the tale is never quite finished.

Deadly silence squelches
the street vendors, the traffic around us.

We toast a young sweet captive
we have only heard about
somewhere in El Territorio
Sur de Baja California.

Leveling

We untangle lawn chairs
get comfortable in the company
of strangers, beer
bracelets on our wrists.

We sip and hear the band on stage
toes begin to tap, shoulders
dipping, we bounce.
Someone gets up to dance,

his blue work cap turned backwards
so as to not bump her pretty nose.
We all watch grinning
kind of like cousins in the barn.

During set changes we speak
without introductions, munch brisket
and potato salad and I can't help
but think how cool real Oklahoma is

or how real, cool Oklahoma is
mixing folks, leveling castes
we thought we needed, a common
blues heartsong. We testify.

We are irreducible witness
insatiable in our longing to be familiar.
I see our scars, our lack
of fashion, the two-dollar sandals

and false gold jewelry,
there is nothing here to pretend.
Black and white dance together:
Mexicans with green

or yellow and orange shirts
Indians wearing turquoise
yuppies fitting in, OU tee shirts
black bras, white shorts and straw hats

cheap sunglasses, sweating flesh
feeling the riffs, feeling songs
we all know like church.

Better than church, everybody grooves

everybody feels, children tug
at skirts, bounce alongside dad
and grandpa whose cigar smoke mingles
with over-priced beer and onion breath.

Gentle dark comes, a train passes
through Bricktown, other folks going
other places while we celebrate
this confessing time.

Pyramids

I've never had a burning desire
to see the Pyramids. It is enough
to know they remain jaunted
and haunted in a desert
on the other side of the world—
symbol of some powerful attempt
to immortalize mortality.

I've always identified with the one
forced to carry the stones
rather than the one cracking the whip
so how can I worship in solace
what my back has carried for another
and how can I walk with my love
into a desert sunset when we are bound
to the whim of a god posing as man—
or worse, a man playing god?

Janitor

His existence is a blues tune
That he wishes could be played
in Memphis, where he visited
on his precious few days off
from cleaning the halls and bathroom
stalls with mop and bucket, his
quiet demeanor masking tunes
only he knows, private riffs,
wrong turns way back when, muddy times
recalled in sweeping rhythms
late at night on a lonely stage.

Flagman on a Road Crew

I did not notice his powder blue jeans,
tar-splashed boots, stained white tee shirt
or burly arms holding the STOP sign
upright as traffic lined up to wait
while his coworkers covered potholes.

I did notice his once-crimson OU cap
now fading to pink in the Oklahoma sun.
He turned the sign to SLOW, and as we
passed I saw vacant eyes aimed
at some distant Saturday in September.

Flapping in Wind

Driving through Alpena
I saw a guy porch-sitting
drinking Mountain Dew
from a two-litter plastic jug.

A faded rebel flag hung
askew in the front window
beside a rusted screen
door flapping in wind.

Passing, I saw his face
close (gearing down
for small-town cops).
I saw his eyes, his red ears.

And he saw me. In that
chance glimpse of recognition
I shifted gears and thanked
God for plastic jugs.

Cigar on Tybee Island

I sit in a broken beach chair
folding beneath me in the sand
while I try to light a cigar
cursing a cheap lighter
fearing the potential peace
of this cigar at sunset
will be wasted—waves
creeping closer to my feet.

I'm about to give up when
two Low-Country lads striding
past notice my predicament.
They approach, ask me
Ya need a torch?

I denounce my cheap lighter
in their presence. They smile
a knowing smile, offer me
instead their high-dollar torch.

My hands shake as I hold
close their polished, prized,
silver-plated tool, trying to light
up as I notice their bizarre tats
blazed above old tennis shoes,
below cut-off denim and
otherwise un-kept appearance.

They grin happy grins, glad
to be helping one find pleasure.
Their pleasant banter tells me
I need a *Good* lighter for Tybee,
politely implies that only a
cheap stranger such as myself

would come here unprepared,
trying to get by for less.

You gotta have a good one
for Tybee—A good one for Tybee—
they repeat three times between
the both of them—as if there
is a secret I should discover,
a flame yet to be lit.

When I Dream

      the branches quicken
green, snow melts, grass
emerges overnight...

when I dream

      policeman don't shoot
us and preachers remain true
to their first love...

when I dream

      color unites us, warms
our cold hands by a fire
glowing small and still

      branches quicken
green, snow melts, grass
flourishes in dark night

when I dream.

Chicago Rain

In August rain
flickers like salt

on young men
in starched shirts

and ties—staples
of the city

like meat turning
on a stick—the

task is to
keep moving.

In Darkness

In darkness
I listen to blues on the radio:
Mississippi John Hurt: "make me
a pallet on your floor"...

Lightning flashes outside, thunder
a short distance away.

Some darkness
is friendly, like a cup of tea.

You learn something
in the dark

               fringes of light.

You write down some words
you hope they like to hear
in New York

           in New York
where darkness never comes
and thunder lingers
like a dream.

Jazz

Strings of an upright bass
bounce at the bidding
of hard fingertips
commanded by a will
that smiles while slapping
a rhythm that bends
the player and the played
into one drama,
a terrible joy
that speaks its own
sorrow—enough that you
and the others feel
some new chaos
syncopating in holy night.

Jouissance (New Orleans)

Eight young males—a couple of trumpets,
two trombones, a baritone, a drum set and cymbals
playing on street corners unannounced.

Karen is now only misty rain, just a tropical
depression that messed up my fishing, but not enough
to squelch the joy on French Market Street.

I am caught up in carnival—follow the gleeful
rhythm these angels calling us to glory. Maybe they
are my messiah I must follow—a happy parade
of penitent-less pilgrims fading in corner shadows.

At last, I decide I cannot follow them forever. I stop
and breathe. Humidity pats me on the back like I passed
some initiation rite, some atavistic union of loose-fitting
atoms collected in a few blissful moments.

It is at this moment,
as the brass ensemble marches into the dreary distance
that suddenly I feel alone...
I look up and see nothing but the close, heavy sky
a blanket over this felt world.

A flash strikes my memory. I see the bright stars
shimmering over my few acres back home, the grand stars
hanging low in black night gripping the earth, its red soil,
the olive leaves, sage grass turning yellow, the Milky Way
glowing like a laser across my back steps.

Rain from this tropical storm may float north and west
to water my home, and then I remember how a solitary
isolated piece of prairie in Pottawatomie County Oklahoma
is connected to this jubilee occurring all around me.

On the Corner: Royal and St. Ann

She strums a mandolin slow
echoes with harmonica,
sings sad-sounding songs.

People pass with just a glance
no crowds, no clapping, no gleeful
street-dancing like other performers
command in this Crescent City.

But she is New Orleans too.

Her isolated performance speaks
to me, a plaintive voice seeking
a home in this world, sweet
melancholy too honest to mask.

I want to wrap her in a package
and send her safely to the place
she has dreamed since a girl standing
before a smudged mirror making
musical sense from questions
that tinged her thoughtfulness.

I want to take her home, give her
a stage, let her understated grace
blossom into something Emmy Lou
and Nancy Griffith would envy.

But the world is not judicious.

But maybe her song endures
because singing truth keeps an unfair
world from grinding to a halt. Her
voice slices the humidity and we listen
and we are carved into particles
that become manageable.

Maybe she sings for those of us
not lucky enough to find the rainbow,
let alone the treasure—those
too preoccupied to face the longings
she makes into melodies
daring to stand in these same streets
where smiling swing bands swagger
keeping happy people hopping.

She is a low-lit lamp on a dark street,
on a dark street that thousands pass,
and her song must not go out
her song must not go out.

A Cocktail Waitress
(whose name I fail to remember)

but her eyes
are pumas
piercing
a tangled mess

pouncing—
dumb boys sidle
up to her.
She ignores

them as long
as she can but
her job requires
a smile

a kind touch
on the arm or shoulder
she passes
holding drinks

aloft
to pacify children
who never
will man her.

But somewhere,
I need to believe,
after the last
superficial

to-do has ended
after tabs and tips
are counted,
somewhere

she stands
before a mirror—
proud lioness
that she is—

slowly strokes
her dark locks,
her blackness,
her white eyes

burning
holes through glass
which could never
hold her.

Roots

Her eyes and hair
are Asian, but
her upward smile
when she sings
shows influence

of the West—
she's been with us
for a while—
singing harmony
to our ballads

in cowboy boots
and a sleeveless
summer dress.
She holds the mic
with one hand

smiles sadly
following the lead
blending
the timeless truth
in folk songs.

East meeting West,
she embodies
good-heartedness
we want in this land,
but still I wonder

about her roots.
Is this home? Or
does some other
voice call her
when she sings

our songs, the way
we want them
sung, as if history
did not happen,
as if life is just a song?

Sunflowers Rising Yellow
Primal and Proud

Train

for LeAnne Howe
after Miko Kings

At 12:26 am, a train softly rumbles
a few blocks from my bed
where I would be sleeping were it not
for a baseball story keeping me up

thinking about Ada, circa 1900, a town
maneuvering toward statehood where
for more than a century now, Iron Horses
have trotted that same path blowing horns

of progress, sometimes too loud to hear
Choctaw ghosts telling of Miko Kings
and our counter-clockwise rotations,

but tonight, soft enough to imagine
old days when baseball meant everything
that money could not buy.

Pastoral: Near Macalester Oklahoma

Brindle cow in the corner of a pasture
on a sunny Sunday morning after three
rainy days cuds the day away, over-
sized eyes matted with springtime mucus,
content after the morning's milking.

She spends hours in solitude giving
of her ragamuffin self to a family—
now tucked away in a church pew down
the road, perhaps remembering to thank
the angels for a friend as dependable

as the crucifix hanging around their necks,
efficacious like the statue on the lawn,
the family saint grazing patiently, knotty
tail switching until vespers, brass bell
dangling from an ungainly neck.

Dusk

The next mountain over
a farmer checks his cows
at dusk riding a four-wheeler.

His light circles the topmost
meadow like his father's
father once did with a lantern

and mule. From here, it all
looks the same. I might as well
be lost at sea or landing

in fog at O'Hare—a soundless
light seeking survivors.
I suppose black cows against

dark trees in darker pastures
are glad to see him loud and clear
—behind that distant light a

man seeks good news, counting
what matters most, steady
as a purring kitten.

Glistening Longhorns

In October dew
curved horns spiral down
to the giving earth,
gentle heads munching
soggy glowing grass
shimmering in sun.

These are not the days
of spooky cattle
driven cross-country
to some unseen place
where cowboys get drunk
and waste their money

after outlasting
the stereotypes
that made epic films—
the myth we cling to
confirming our taste
for making heroes

from splintered dust
and desperate pilgrims.
On this gentle slope
these quiet giants
graze a life that cowboys
might should envy.

A Bell

I'm not certain why I return
to childhood standing
between twin cedars
at the end of a short sidewalk
in front of the pink house
a few feet of concrete leading
away, out toward the dust
and prairie wind.

An old bell hung there
on a cedar post
and for some reason I liked
to be close to that heavy note
that called us home.

More than once I got in trouble
for ringing too often
or at the wrong time—the value
of its sound was found
in timely usefulness.

Even then, the bell seemed to be
a symbol beyond itself,
its power felt in its silent, motionless
existence—what it could say
if called upon.

All these years later, I hear
an uncle inherited the bell.
It no longer hangs at the old house
that now has new siding, a new roof
and windows—but the house still sits
on the same knoll, the walk leading
away, out toward the dust
and prairie wind.

Somewhere, somewhere
that bell continues—it could not rust
in three lifetimes—its ringing
will never go unheard.

Of Men and Machinery

he slipped a cog

he said to euphemize
unbearable pain

and I thought the sound
of his words
were so eloquently
anachronistic

that I wished for that time
when machinery
was simple
the days young when

the loss we now feel
was not imaginable...

no one plows or builds
with failure in mind,
but thus is the nature
of men and machinery...

Old Man Henry

I.

Eat off your old man
as long as you can;
Eat off your old man
as long as you can

He repeated his advice. It came
in pairs to me from this curious
evocator alone in western Oklahoma,
who rode the rails west out of
Tennessee—depression-era going
somewhere, anywhere—motion
is always better than hunger,
motion is better than hunger.

II.

He must have been past eighty
when he took a liking to me, his
lean, tall frame like a fine walking
horse only lately cherished

                    this
gentleman who now enjoyed living
out his newfound role as sage
of Woods County.

                    He'd been there
long enough to remember with wisdom
where it was he came from—*Tennessee*
just the way he said it sounded honeyed,
ephemeral, no longer binding

not to be
confused with the here and now—this
place of red dirt and opportunity for miles
as far as an eye can see—this place where he,
for reasons he cannot name, got off the train
and dug in.

III.

I'm just a big boy that summer.
I'm making good money
in the hayfield and catching catfish
at night—sprawled on a Canadian River
sandbar, yellow poles nine feet high
sticking up out of sand, we look hard
at the tips tipping in starlight, a fire dim
behind us, a stringer-full splashing
at water's edge.

                I am eighteen
and every Sunday morning at the church
door Old Man Henry shakes my hand
and repeats his mantra:

Eat off your old man
as long as you can;
Eat off your old man
as long as you can

                —his eyes misty
with sincerity, his hands so large,
tender—but oh so large.

Great Grandpa Gustava

He was conscripted into the Kaiser's army once
before, so when they came knocking a second
time, he married Julia and got the hell out
of their Hungarian home, took a honeymoon

trip to Ellis Island, never to return. He was
a crack shot, but in Oklahoma he preferred
to walk pastures every day calling his cows
by name, recording their refugee lives

flourishing in buffalo grass and gyp water
flowing through Greenleaf Creek. His collar
was buttoned to the top, a pipe curling
from his chapped lips rested on his chest.

For Julia, he translated the newspaper to
Hungarian, but refused to speak to salesmen
or unwanted visitors: *No English. Talk boy*
he would say pointing to one of seven sons.

After so much nonsense, he would bark
his custom cryptic phrase: *Go to hell, shit!*
Thus ending the exchange, thus keeping
a capricious world from tipping out of balance.

Homecoming
for Uncle Max

Greed, I guess—my father answered
me uncharacteristically critical
of our ancestors, their impulsive
move to New Mexico Territory

stopping somewhere around Clayton
where nothing worked out. When
the horses died from grazing locoweed
they loaded their sparse selves in a wagon

and bleakly headed back to northwest
Oklahoma—the grass in those Gypsum
Hills green enough. They returned
to what they feared, reclaimed what they

knew, relinquished a short-lived dream
busted now like clods of red clay
crumbling to dust beneath a cattle herd.
It's not easy to feed seven growing boys

so the toughest, Uncle Arnold, walked
back—herding the cattle as he made way
all those miles along unmarked paths
primal as a Kalahari Bushman—big boy,

keeper of the family's future swaying,
stumbling, shitting slowly toward home
through cactus and redrock steadfast
under sun and stars close enough to touch.

Worship Hour

In Lakeview Texas
(population 152
and no lake in sight)

bare stalks line
plowed cotton fields
in sienna-colored soil.

Deserted homesteads
windmills and irrigators
piped across fields

giant green tractors
stand on guard
tattered cotton scraps

float along ditches.
Just three pickups
wait at the door

of the Baptist Church,
a faithful few gathered
for God's word.

A picture of Jesus
hangs behind the pulpit
in a sanctuary

where crowds gathered
back when cotton
was picked by hand.

Texas Swing

In Turkey Texas

A pickup rolls like molasses
from the Methodist Church
diagonally down street
to the Sunday diner.

At the intersection another
pickup waits: a white-haired,
mustached cowboy with his bride
by his side, turns even slower.

They both wave to me here
in the home of Bob Wills
where a three-dollar museum
waits the occasional visitor.

I guess old Bob got these folks
used to celebrity life, strangers
and all, swinging through.

Silverton Texas

Up from Caprock Canyon
I shake clay from my boots,
say hello to strangers who
puzzle at my lime green kayak
holstered to my pickup.

There's not much water here
but today it's raining steady.
I just want to be prepared
in case the water gets high
I tell them, and they chuckle.

Inside, sipping coffee, I slide
my boots across wood floors,
the original grain rubbed fine
by years of scooting—ochre
trim boards, dust-colored walls.

Cowboy decor hanging about
the place is upstaged by two recent
photos placed behind the cash
register: one frames six cheerleaders,
the other, fifteen football players

(plus a student manager in a white
pressed shirt). Chests thrusting,
numbered for all time, they do
locals proud, bearing witness to
strangers passing through.

Taqueria Jalisco Restaurante
Lubbock, Texas

They have a welcoming feel
despite quick glances
at the strange, large gringo
when he first enters, seated,
stumbles some Spanish.

Coffee and Mexican breakfast
makes him feel patron-like—
the uplift of community—
young girls in green and black
serving old men, laughing.

It's Saturday morning so they
have barbacoa—he orders four
tacos *con cilantro y cebolla*—
eats quietly, his senses adrift
—*que sabroso! Muy sabroso.*

Red brick columns, orange
and lime flowers, pink flamingos,
frescos from another world live
before us—*la musica* begins,
a tragic baritone, traditional Latin

rhythms keeping score—the ice
machine squeaking in the kitchen,
a dust pan bumping rock-tile floor
swept perpetually by a young man
defined by the dignity of work.

Texas Rain

The super-sized sky full
of boiling blue clouds
peppers gray dust
with trillions of rain drops.

Near Amarillo you
start to hope again
and pray the radiator
doesn't blow.

Some Texans are the finest
people you've known
anywhere—some
are not. It's just that you

have driven these same roads
so long you forget
you know other roads,
other worlds. Things change

so fast—temperature,
pressure, wind—only
the road seems the same.
Like everything

rain will not last. Change,
in this country full
of Confidence Men, swoops
like a Broad-Shouldered

Hawk hunting on the draft
of a brewing storm
leading you down the road.
You feel bigger

this afternoon, as long
as the engine holds
and the wipers clear
your vision. You see

miles on miles and fear not
the unexpected.
East of Dallas you
grow tired, start looking

for a place to bed down,
wonder about a farmhouse
with a yard light
near bending Oak.

East of Austin

There is a wildness unknown
to hippies or yuppies
a place of broken settlements
beside a few surviving homesteads
with tattered windmills
where strong people endure
work in hot sun, echo a time
before the Alamo before Goliad
or Gonzalez, a place where time
seems incidental, where mesquite
and live oak and prickly pear
mark a landscape, a place
where longhorns and goatherds
graze alongside white birds.

A Herd of Antelope, Extraordinarily Beautiful
after Chekhov, Ward No. 6

When the prayers have ended
other are just begun.

The days inside
and the time outside
may really be the same

but where then is the source of dreams?
What do the dying see
that the living overlook?

Except for beauty too little
considered and grace, rarely perceived

dying is to be alive
even as living is dying.

On New Mexico's table land
I have seen a herd of antelope,
extraordinarily beautiful
and graceful
                              the sun
in the morning glimmers,
silver singing between us.

I sigh,
sigh for them, for us all.

As you pray, remember,
even God runs with the herd.

Native Flute
for Erny Zah

In the closing distance
feel pulse
behind the woodwind

melody bathed
in sweetness
like honeysuckle at dawn.

Mourn the loss
by playing today—
cherish the hope

of this time—
sit still and let wind
teach its way.

Dance
in the corridor of souls
looping

toward tomorrow
and fear no evil.
Play on—

blow the breath
of solidarity,
your wind

catching flight
with eternal breath
fingers soft

on reeds springing
deep from earth.
Oh joy! Oh hope!

Prescilianos Café: Cuba, New Mexico

It's not a morning for talking
only two others in the café.

I whisper my order—burrito
with green chili. She pours
coffee with a faint smile
no flirting, no banter.

It's quiet, like the valley
beneath the green mountains
under a crystal sky.

She's a diligent worker,
mixed-race, fair skin, hazel eyes,
canyon-blonde hair.

She wears long red earrings,
a white ruffled top,
black nylon pants, sandals

and when she speaks
her accent gently clinks
against my ear like ice
in a glass of summer tea,

no ring on her finger
no cross on her neck.

Driving from Bloomfield
south on 550 through
remote landscape dotted
with yellow-tipped sage

broomweed, juniper, dusty
mesas in the distance,

ochre and broad against
blue sky and puffy clouds

you feel the descent
into this sleepy village
shaded by mountains.

It's time for breakfast
time to sit quietly
in a vinyl booth
notice wood beams above

sip coffee and remember
the trout you caught
the osprey overhead
while you stood numb
in the clear cold water.

Take another sip,
feel the sadness in her eyes
beyond the smile.

Lean back, stretch
your stream-weary legs
and begin to think
about the long road ahead.

When O'Keeffe Found a Skull

the world did not change
but we did. Only we
could place a rose
where once a brain
responsive to instinct

dwelt just to be tamed.
Never have we understood
wildness bending us.
Gawking at the museum
or drifting

in the desert, bending
is the ultimate gesture.
Art is nothing
but bleaching sun,
the transfiguration

of wind recording
for the sake of time—sand
covering our feet, dead
gas deep in night—darkness
streaming as light.

Our Lady of Guadalupe Church:
Navajo Dam Community, New Mexico

Endless sky makes me feel
forever is possible
but now we frame
infinity in walls—

plastered and steepled.
A wrinkled belfry
calls out to desert
all around—blue sky,

red rim rock, green juniper,
dusty purple sage.
The faithful follow
a clanging iron bell

harsh-waking a hushed land
where life sobers
beneath sovereign sun.
They leave chores to walk

slowly past a crystal stream
shadowed by yellow
cottonwood up and down
rugged mesas

following a bell ringing
everlasting air
with no regard for person
or office—a clarion

call—indifferent yet
irresistible.
Even rocks cry out
echoing our souls

tethered to such stern signals
of mortality
ringing hard—long
after sound has ceased.

San Juan Relief: Yellow Blooms Early in March

I'm a hundred miles down the road
from that one spot in the trout stream
where I stand transfixed, the water
hypnotizing me as I concentrate
on the fly and the hunted fish.

My only respite is to look up
resting my eyes on a low bluff
bordering the stream, covered
with sage grass in yellow bloom.

The rust-red rock, the dusty green
stems, sandy yellow flowers
in subtle relief, my eyes look up
to dull blue sky, charcoal clouds.

Two hundred, five hundred miles
down the road driving toward duty
that unnamed boulder endures
just above the river—yellow flowers
blooming wild early in March.

Chanson d' aventure:
New Mexico Railrunner Express

Traveling north
to Santa Fe
by light rail
rising across
plateaus, junipers
cottonwoods,

snow-covered
mountains frame
this gentle ride
until we come
to Santa Fe
where despite

the bright air
sidewalk minstrels
and bold church bells
I stop cold
before O'Keeffe's
abrupt vision

titled *A Street*—
a city scape
without green
where even sun
struggles to land—
a diminished

lamp loiters
low and obscure
at street's end.
The painting haunts
me hours later
riding home

as sun sets
on this wilderness
on land free
from concrete,
land she loved
speaking still.

The Poets' Lament

We feel it deeply—
this helpless feeling
that we cannot save

anything worth saving
save our voice
raised in praise of beauty

the goodness of life—
the feeling we get
driving 285 south

Santa Fe to Clines Corner
on a bright August morning,
the various shades

of green mingled
on the caprock,
the rust-colored arroyos

sunflowers rising yellow
proud and primal
in ultimate protest.

Like Vagrant Birds Fluttering above a Fencerow

Tire Swing

It hangs from a Cottonwood near Mud Creek.
I'm surprised this tiny outlet has a name
although now the muddy water
is bruised with oil sludge.

The tire swing hangs limp.
The frowning Cottonwood remembers
times when a young dad strung the rope
and tied a bald tire in place.

A fun-making dad, adored
by his child swinging on summer afternoons,
Oklahoma wind lifting
the tire, the boy squeaking in delight.

Both are gone now:
An old man hardly remembers anything
except debt, foreclosure
and a dream that never woke.

The boy sits in an office cubicle
in Duncan keeping Halliburton
relevant. His tours of duty
in Iraq, his weekend warrior-ship

are the closest things now
to childhood adventure—those first days
swinging strong, flying high
above Mud Creek—free and clear.

At Roman Nose Sate Park

Beneath a Cottonwood
I pitch a tent—
wait on afternoon to sift
away, wind swooshing specks of time
through leafy trees, sweat
drops sticking to my shirt

Sometimes I think I hear
ghosts from centuries past
when following bison mattered most
those primal days
marked by bird and beast
that too soon gave way to a cow path
cutting across prairie

Not far from here yellow wheat
is harvested with red or green combines
white trucks haul grain to elevators
conspicuously raised on the prairie—
some place that became sort
of a town, some railroad stop
marking progress

Beneath a Cottonwood
I pitch a tent—
wait on afternoon to drift
away, wind swooshing specks of time
through leafy trees, sweat
drops sticking to my shirt.

Black-Capped Chickadee

The professor circles to the back
of a classroom where students
struggle with a poem:
Speaking by Simon J. Ortiz.

Making his rounds, he sees
a bird upside down, feeding
on a pod of Maple seeds
outside the classroom window

and for a few lyrical seconds
is translated into bliss.
He mentions it to the group
perched near the window

calls them to see what he sees,
names it for them,
and though they seem
relieved to look up

from the assigned poem,
how quickly they smile
dismissing the old bird,
completely missing the point.

Too soon these fledglings
will be robed and capped
and scattered loose
in a world upside down

where professors fade
in bleak September dust
and poems, like birds, hang
on, waiting to be sung.

Interruption
for Rilla

A Phoebe built her nest
under the fascia on the porch
an arm's length away.

Each time I go to the door
she flees the nest in panic
circles to nearby limbs

keeping a wary eye on me.
At times I wish I were a bug
so she could gobble me

then return to nest in peace.
But then I would not hear Pan
fluting in the forest, or see

a shepherd boy gently fifing
on the giant fieldstone
beneath sheltering Oak limbs.

How then would the Muse
find me and harmonize
melody with mystery?

Crow Stepping through Wet Grass on a Rainy Morning

Even this old sailor is tired of water.
Down from his lofty perch, sadly
pecking his way through soggy grass,
he shakes off muddy clay clinging
to his claws. The black sheen of his coat
is dulled in drizzle this moist morning
when all earth seems compromised,
its texture mushy, its color blanding
to gray. His cloudy, downcast eyes
betray his limitations, while a fateful
sea rises, drenching, saturating us
with mortality—his cocky voice now
quiet. This is no time for crowing.

River in Morning

A man sits riverside
every morning early in the breeze
in the first strokes of sunlight,
the latent moon.

He watches water flow by him
as if he is watching nothing
the water never ceasing
moving past him

quiet except for the occasional splash
or rise along the rocks.
The man, this water, this ritual
of non-doing, this act

of non-being, erasing
a lifetime of senseless toil
removing a world where all things
rob us, take us away

so nothing is left
except the patient desire to see
what he has never before seen
what he has never allowed himself to be.

White River Repose

In a thirty dollar hotel room
one night by the White River
after hard fishing in winter wind

we read Walt Whitman aloud,
pausing now and again to discern
the Muse listening close, old

lines echoing off torn yellow walls,
worn carpet, a brown table,
particle board dressers and lumpy

mattresses with stained pillows.
Song of the Open Road follows us
home – like fallow fields at dusk.

Death on a River

I would like to believe
most of them were not aware
of those cruel seconds
between living and dying

before the sun was warm
when a blitzkrieg of lethal
water ambushed sleepy
camps, entombing so many

tented, bed-rolled, shrouded
for their dust-covered graves, once
the flash flood recedes so
their sopped bodies can be found.

When I was a Heron

I stalked the slippery shallows
as quiet as a falling star.
I hated the motorized boats
crisscrossing the rocky currents.
I did my fishing close to shore
near those dead overhanging logs.
I waited with a perfect eye,
and with precise timing I speared
the fish, graciously unaware.

It was those days when I was young
when the stars did not disappear
though the barn light burned and kitchen
candles flickered until pink dawn.
There was plenty; there was restraint.
It was then you head me squawking
as the sun dropped into gray hills
and I knew darkness, like all things
good, was nothing to keep.

Whippoorwill

Calling from the underbrush
in perfect cadence this poet
of the hardwoods sings
what some refuse to hear.

Evening stars appear, moonlight
trickles through limbs, lays
gentle on the sloping prairie.

I have some lines of my own
but why should I interrupt
the sublime, so out of style
with so many pundits?

Evening is clear and calm.
A few fireflies light the way
above solemn shadows.

The storms of yesterday
seem so far removed.
Dark and light balance
what we find so hard to find.

Rituals at Dusk

A cigar at sundown after supper
sipping a glass of rose wine
as the wind settles

A doe lollops in clover
where Prairie Pentstemon stands
at the edge of the yard

A few birds chase flies
in the calm before Whippoorwills
and tree frogs chant darkness full.

These are the days of green
repose, of evening bliss
before summer simmers down.

These are ceremonies you keep:
simple, smoky intercession
savored once again.

Fallen

Walnut leaves fallen
on my truck window
last night's rain
brought them down.

This morning I smell
the sharp odor of walnut
skin broken, the smell
of autumn—good

memories of an Ozark
childhood where
even the toughest timber
had its time to die.

Autumn Reprise

The edge of a wheat field
sun streaming the west
beneath a hackberry
in sage grass and ragweed
fallen cottonwood scattered

a muzzleloader leans
against a fence post, barb wire
stringing an empty sky—
an empty field—
red dirt aside

Raindrops on a Plastic Coffee Lid

Brown coffee spots beside tiny drops
of rain—I can never keep coffee
from spilling onto the lid, down
the corner of my mouth, the front
of my shirt.

I am sitting along the Mississippi
looking at the bridge, the morning sun,
clouds that sprinkle my chicory coffee,
so welcome this morning.

I wonder if I were native to New Orleans
would I be a poet, would lines follow me here
all the way downstream to this dramatic ending
that begins what we call the Gulf of Mexico?

I think the colors of the French Quarter
would inflame me, certainly the horns
and the bass lines would move me, but I
might have to take a boat ride, drift
toward the sea to find the soul of all
that we see, all that we sense.

So easy to forget how water comes
to us, how tourists drinking next door
are related to brown pelicans perched
on poles just a few miles from here,
these misremembered brethren, these
brown ambassadors who take flight
only when closely threatened, even
then fleeing with a curious dignity.

New Orleans is impressionistic.
Everything blurs, everything blends,
the whole is what matters. We are all
drops of color on discovered canvass.

I like how no one seems to be judged.
If your hair is blue, that's cool. If it's fire
orange or corn-rowed, or balding, who gives
a damn? If you wear a wheat beard down
to your navel, well that's just fine. Shades
of skin, such a big deal in so many places,
here, only seem to brighten the picture.
The dialects, the accents, the phrases spice
the pot. We are all tumbling notes in jazz
riffs that never want to end.

One guy rides a double-decker bicycle
through Rue Royal ten feet above us.
If you want to be alone on a bicycle made
for two, or a couple on a single bike,
that's just grand. Did you see the shorts
and the boots? Did you notice the colors
of the hats, the blouses? Color, Color
everywhere and none of it is wrong.

Hear the troupe of young troubadours
walking the street—a gang with horns
and drums and a cardboard box for tips.
These guys got the whole street swinging!
How natural their rhythm sways, how good
to see young males smiling, joyful in the art
of making music, giving strangers a gift,

giving themselves purpose, happy to express
their ancestors' pain through the power glide
of a trombone, the close fingering of a trumpet,
syncopated double time of a hollow drum
come to life while tourists try to dance
and take photos in dim street light.

And out there, a few blocks away, those
brown pelicans sit tight in the comfortable
night—a knowing look fixed on their faces.

A Savior Dressed in Yellow

Saint Rachel, pray for us.
Forgive us, though we know
what we do.

Here on the edge
of small-town America
in the heart of "God's Country"
on the outskirts of the one universe
we claim to know
women drop used diapers
in the Wal-Mart parking lot,
wanna-be fishermen leave beer cans,
plastic bottles and Styrofoam worm boxes
on riverbanks. Here, neighbors
put plastic bags of trash on the edge
of the lawn where every stray dog and cat
scatters the contents up and down the streets.

Here on the edge
of small-town America
in the heart of "God's Country"
on the outskirts of the one universe
we claim to know
a man wearing lime-striped tennis shoes,
a yellow shirt and clashing off-yellow hat
spends Sunday mornings wielding
his home-made stick-with-a-nail-in-the-end-of-it
picking up our trash.

Saint Rachel, pray for us.
Can you forgive us, since we know
what we must—
and what we must not do?

Arcing

The arc is reality
as far as we know.
The question
is to discern
where you are
in orbit.

The hunter hoses
blood out
of his pickup bed
and for the moment
circles above
vulture-like

though
we might say
he is more hunted
than he knows.

Bear Dreams

Silent bears perplex
my dreams, appear
from the shadows
in hunter green forests
as dusky sun slants
upright firs and pines
on a pungent brown
path I follow deep
into woods.

Sometimes I watch
them from a cautious
distance, shaking
with fear in underbrush.

Sometimes I shoot
at them, always missing
the vitals, inciting
a ferocious attack.

Fleeing in terror
I marvel at their power,
amazed that I stumble
across their secret
existence.

Blue River Lion

Walking slowly downhill
yellow sun dissipating
through brown leaves, my bow
dangling useless at my side

I'm wondering why I saw
no deer, when suddenly
before me, 500 feet below
a full-grown lion stalks

across my very path
moving sure without haste,
hunting—his tawny skin
vibrating over taut muscles

a four-foot tail curling
menacingly above his back
the silence is like thunder—
there is no stillness like this.

Stopped, I cannot move.
I have never been so close
to pure violent beauty.
I am dumb-struck with terror.

Going Home

On Interstate 35 north
of Guthrie, driving through
evening shadows I pass
a rusting, stale green Chevy
bouncing along on bald tires
with a great antlered deer
tied across the tattered roof.

I see a good Oklahoma boy
driving grateful, his eyes geared
straight ahead toward home
where his bride and kids await
his arrival with meat for winter,
stories to tell, hope for better
days ahead strapped tight
to the wildness in our souls.

Winter

Days are shorter
than I want.

My cousin Bear
told me to prepare

but I was fooled
by crows at dawn

who come and go
as they please.

I am a building
a nest in the dark.

Amid the Trees

Into the Garden now come we all
aghast and grieving
for the sake of knowledge
the burden of inquiry never leaving
us tame, the cloud-covered moon
ghostly white amid the trees
forlorn—the center bark—the touch
no one can overcome, the verdict
no jury overturns—and I,
columned like so many sheep
in the stall condemned, await
the glory of the Lord shining
all around telling me what we
have so eagerly found out on our own.

Mystery

There's nothing new here:
It is older than the Garden
itself—a man sitting within earshot
of crows, hearing the eternal song
run again through his memory

a spring bubbling unexpectedly
up and grass bending all
around the breeze humming
that familiar tune in the afterglow
of death—friends come and go.

We speculate their new existence.
We long for their presence
in their absence, the heart
grasping anything—the great
uphill climb continues

and becoming honest, we
become divine—the acorns
fall to earth, grass bends
accepting them—the crows
keep time—the song endures.

Nomadic Sky

Looking across prairie grass
green in mid-day sun,
orange flowers sprinkled
through a pasture
bending in soft breeze
under nomadic sky
I ask myself: *Is this
the place where I will die?*

How we float between
wind-blown seeds
and dirt-covered roots,
but looking at the world
through the eyes of a flower
I see nothing is ultimate,
I am always, only
contingent.

Like vagrant birds fluttering
above a fencerow,
I can't help but value
a place that welcomes me
to lay down roving
and die—the way earth
prefers—settled in the core
of the unnamed.

Blades of Conformity

A Road

I lay down with thunder,
pines whistle above me.
A tiredness takes over
like waves upon the sand.

I see the good of my
life is not mine at all—

as Chuang Tzu observes:
*A road is made by people
walking on it*—and a poem,
like a life, is drafted
at the mercy of that
which is unseen.

Words

I believe in words
like I believe in the smile
of a pretty girl.

Once it was everything.
There was nothing else,
nothing to question.

Now words, like bath water
dripping, are forgotten
as the day passes.

I've read the linguists,
philosophers and theologians.
I believe in the words of Gods

all of them, and sitting
in moonlit darkness I notice
the bright distant stars

that seem permanent,
have faded while the earth turns,
spinning time

and the memory of wise
or witty phrases vanish
on the horizon.

I believe in words
when I hear my countrymen
rationalize illogical

incomplete pronouncements
of preachers, pundits
and politicians.

Then I withdraw into silence.
What can you say to intentional,
irrational misrepresentation?

Words tease, words wound,
cut us to pieces.
I believe them; and I tremble.

When finally I rise to go inside
and call it a night
I see the elm tree fully leafed

outlined in darkness
and know that in the morning
it will still be standing

where I left it. The early sun
reveals at least this consistent,
deep-rooted growth.

It may not last forever,
but forever is a long, long time.
So I will keep on saying

and I will keep on listening,
the leaves folded like prayer
through this night of darkness.

Hunger

One night I built a fire
in my backyard.

I got so lonely
I went in the house,
got two ears of corn,
wrapped them in foil,
placed them in the fire

then tonged them out,
half-hot, unwrapped them
in darkness and ate
kernel by kernel
as if we were best friends,
melted butter dripping
out of my mouth.

Isn't it something
what hunger will do?

Something New

The moon that was so bright
and so full in eastern sky
now shines equally bright
and full in the morning west.

A night has come and gone.

The great light in night sky
shows this spinning globe
by which we mark time
by which we grow old
in constant motion.

We remember that rising moon
glowing above trees
as day ended and dusk arrived.

We remember the night
but wake to something new—

the way it has always been
and no memory can change that.

Blue
for Tim Tingle

A rainy blue night
the car wheels sound
oddly soothing, jazz
horn sweeping low

I drive through heavy sky
as if on the other side
someone knows me,
as if morning will call

my name. At the gate
I pause, feel the steel
chain in my palm, turn
the key—empty trees,

dead grass, always.
Somewhere, someone
on a small boat at sea
stands on deck, sniffs

silent air, as I do now.
My lungs fill with cedar
and humidity. I think
about many things.

A Few Days after the Funeral

Only silence remains
absence follows everywhere
awaits my arrival
rides my back—I bend
broken, dull, everything
seems plastic if not ephemeral
peaches are sour
salt has no savor
I'm losing weight unaware.

What I would give
for some chatty well-wisher
to say *God Bless You*
one more time—so I could smile
and hate them for their concern,
for their piety, so I could nod
numbly and stare blank-eyed
at the collar of their white shirt
or black blouse.

I want to hear them clear their throats,
stumble at their words again.

It's too much, it's too much
to hear a boy's laughter
to undo the dying—so anything,
anything to drive out this damn silence.

Night Sounds

The voice of an owl perforates night air.

I hear it, feel it while Miles Davis plays
indoors, and I think of two sounds,
two dimensions—out there, in here.

I am remembering what I have forgotten.

Death hovers in the night air: sulking
alive, breathing, penetrating—

the artist is always cringing under
the weight of death—a song
that everyone knows, tunes
we keep hoping to forget.

There is music we often fail to discern.
There must be, there must be.

A Night like This

The earth seems to stand still.
Coyotes bark, a neighbor's dog
and stars above—what stars
we have, we have—and I
want them all. On nights
like this blue stem, belly high
in the field, is silent, no wind
every slight sound is heard:
a fish splash at the pond edge
a screen door squeaks—

I want the stars, the post oaks
tall and serene, I want it all,
want to know it all, be it all.
Fallen leaves crackle
beneath my boots. My dog
walks a little quieter, more light
on his feet. He hears the coyotes
too—we both stop to listen
and I think we both know
what we are listening for.

My breath plumes, mixes
with cigar smoke. I lean
against an oak—on a night
like this I want to forgive
so many things—if I could
just find the right star.

Winter Moon

In close sky above bare Maple
limbs, frigid lines frame
a winter moon, an imperfect,
squashed circle waning,
as we see in early light.

The birds are quiet, the wind
is still, the cold bears down
with force enough to kill, only
the glow of a plaintiff moon
signals a living eye. We

wait at a window, a first cup
of coffee in hand, peer through
slanted, horizontal blinds
across bending, upright limbs
that mark an endless array

of angles. From a space safe
inside we feel the pattern
somehow includes us, if only
in its ability to slow our steps
and to hold our eyes.

Abiding

Thelonius Monk, *Abide*
with Me—a cigar,
a winter storm, my brother
in surgery in Houston
after driving all night
after two weeks of failed remedies
after sleepless anxiety,
the unspoken, interior fight
of faith and reason—the shock
of shock—but now the saxophone
climbs, soaring in jubilation,
the melancholy piano
underscores it all—helpless
but for prayer we wait alone
a long way away, snowed-in,
taking comfort as best we can,
like songbirds flapping in icy wind
seeking berries to sustain us,
contour feathers surviving—
Abide with Me—*Abide*
with Me—cigar smoke wafting
towards eternity.

At Forty Six

She doesn't know if she's young
or not. Some days seem like twenty
some days she envies
grandmothers in their eighties.

They call her in for a biopsy
tell her it's the worst kind
they'll hit it with all they've got
It'll take a miracle—they say.

At forty six she has a daughter
to raise, a husband to love:
mortgage, career, friends, dinners,
flowers, books and songs.

Her mother went fast at sixty seven
and they all said she was much too young
but today twenty years seem gracious
as she prays: *Not now, God,
Not now, Not at forty six.*

How It All Started

Are you like me, do you need
to know why? Do you toss
and turn until a cause is named

assuming that finding cause
will fix it, not understanding
arrogance masking as help?

This is how it all started, this
refusal to accept, this overturning
pride, this way of (not) seeing.

Expectations

At the back of the island where two streams meet
at sunset we come together and kiss slow
the first time, shivering in damp moist air, arms
clutching each other and the flyrods upright,
purple water pressing our legs, the rising
moon slipping behind clouds the last thing I saw
before closing my eyes to taste ecstasy,
trout odor mingling with my sweat and her tired
fragrance, honeysuckle cleansing beyond it
all in the cusp of nightfall until we know.
Withdrawing in timid anticipation
we turn upstream and walk the long way back
across the river to the mainland to a
camp where others are expecting our return.

Zen and the Sensitive Redneck

He's always been good at stacking things.
As a boy he volunteered to stack firewood,
picking up scattered logs, ordering them
to ricks. He made money as a teen by stacking
hay, bucking alfalfa and prairie grass
onto the truck, then into the barn,
marrying the rows tight to last.

He's good at fixing things too.
He repairs fences, wires circuits,
times his engines.

He stacks, he fixes, he builds.
He does these things alone.
The mystery of happiness eludes him
so he finds joy in things:
in wood, in hay, in metal.

His yes is yes, and he means it.
His no means no.

He gave up desire when the pain
scared him, offered him strange visions
he did not understand,
illusions he could not manage.

His life is a tradeoff—he won't desire
and she won't return,
so things occupy his time.

His life is to find joy in a tractor motor
firing on a frosty morning
to feel twine tight on a bale made last summer
to keep fences from sagging

to hear quail calling
to see cattle grazing.

He knows he can depend on grass
and rain and soil—
the satisfaction of partnering
with all these things.

Morning Chore

The sun is up
but I only see
brazen blue clouds
falling dark.

Thunder is all
I hear filling
the valley with
orange lightning.

The immediacy
of things confronts
the senses,
qualifies happiness.

The pinnacle
of our love
was also
the peak of our lie.

Like a dance
we kept time
smiling like fools
across the floor.

I rise to check
horses and cattle,
in every herd
one disrupts a union.

In My Father's House

I.

It's 6:30 in the morning. The sky
has been light for forty minutes
and my father still has not risen
from bed. I don't recall him ever
sleeping late—he's always up
before first light—cup of coffee
in hand looking east, thinking,
praying—being still before
the coming day, the rising sun.

II.

I am the only one awake. I pour
myself a cup of coffee. I use
the "Generic Coffee Mug"—a black
and white novelty present I gave
dad way back in 8th grade—my
middle school witticism collected
alongside many other cups inscribed
with clever slogans, pieces of advice
or life messages to consider.

III.

I am awake and I write these lines
on scratch paper left over from our
card game last night—my doodling
and score-keeping traceable—a ledger
accounting the bid, winner and loser.

IV.

A rare cold front drove us inside
to play cards—to make memories
like Christmas or Thanksgiving—
those winter days when, no matter
how late the games lasted, still dad
would be the first awake, sipping
coffee before dawn, thinking
about his house-full of family.

V.

Now that his grandson is married,
in bed in the next room, maybe dad feels
like he has reached a point in life
where scouting sunrise is not everything.
Maybe joy keeps him warm in bed.
Maybe now he no longer fears the howl
of the working poor, or the graceful
strength of the persistently broken.

Maybe now, he has the luxury
of sleeping late—but it feels wrong
—feels soft—seems like a subtle
loss of control—as if he's an unaspiring
patriarch of a family that gets hyped
on table games and strong coffee,
a family that finds meaning in sunrise.

VI.

The green of the morning is breathtaking.
Despite the cold snap and gray clouds,
the oaks are filled with new leaves, grass
is ankle high, wild flowers pepper
the pasture. The world is alive and well,
if a bit sluggish and gray this morning.

VII.

And why am I up? Why am I writing?
Recording impressions, taking note
of my own mortality—in my father's
house at the table where the cards
have been shuffled and dealt thousands
of times before the bay window
where we have held our coffee in anecdotal
mugs, looked through the window out
to the green, past the green, into a horizon
spilling beyond comprehension.

Coffee Cycle

More than once we woke up
to find strange men asleep
on our couch. We did not ask
but were told to keep quiet.

Smoking was a sin, but dad
let them when they woke
and poured cup after cup
of black coffee down them.

I began to realize black coffee
was God's blood that cured men
so they could go home without
beating their wives and kids.

I worshipped coffee, praised
its aroma wafting from the sanctuary
—my dad a shaman who raised
yellow-skinned, hollow-

toothed drunks from despair,
sent them back to work
cleansed of the Devil's brew—
until the next go round.

Make Do

One day one boy got on
the school bus wearing
blue cowboy boots.

We asked him about
his "new" boots and he
told us his daddy got
them at the dump,
brush-painted them blue.

I wonder if this has ought
to do with the fact
that the same boy
used to piss on the white
church wall every Sunday
after service

a communion we
did not understand.

Yellow School Bus

On rainy mornings too
the big bus crawls
to a squeaky stop
the creaking sound
of a door opening
a strange yellow world.
Cautiously you climb
the stairs one step
at a time, like a puppy
lost in a crowded pen
your eyes careen
confusing horizons
scanning here or there
until the driver's call
—your father's hand
touching you forward.

To Our Children

Don't give up the dream
of tender mercy, requisite
justice—do not be
intimidated by those
who want to change you
into beasts, who entice
you into senseless fights,
indulgent fantasies
of war—no one wins
a "civil" war.

You can only hope
for the daily humble
persistence of a river—
some water rushes
with extroverted power
foaming, careening—
other moves slowly
calmly—but all water
gets to the sea
and the sea welcomes
us all as one, indiscriminately
bathed in the redemption
we only hear talk about,
the cleansing for which we
instinctively yearn.

Our choice: to be led
by absurdity, withering
in self-righteous fear
and illogical bombardment
of the senses—or seek
the glow of humanity
moving undeterred

toward the great and godly
waters that welcome
and pardon us all,
even those sometimes stuck
in blood-spilled banks
along the way.

A Short Poem

I wish I could write
a short poem everyone
would remember.

I might say: *Blessed*
are the merciful
for they shall obtain mercy

but that is already too long,
too literal—
words floating in air

without image,
needing a body, a life
to incorporate.

Old Buddha pointed
to a flower
but how can flowers bloom

when the soil
is choking on words
we refuse to hear?

Windless

Windless, and so full of hope,
the drooping sails
wrinkled together like rummage
have forgotten their purpose
though we sit at sea
days away from port of call.

What are we to do with ourselves
when the wind refuses,
when the breeze fails to comfort
our parching tongues,
when nothing fills our sails
leaving us exiled so far from home?

Is it enough to have boarded ship,
enough to have left the safety
of dry land? Or will ambition
diminish to despair, our good
effort evaporate? Will we be
forgotten, withering, in windless sun.

Settling

a little gold fish
circles
in a transparent bowl
circles
within the limits
of a world he did not make
circles
in a glass trap
that displays his captive self
circles
then finally settles
to the bottom
alone
confined
to what he cannot escape
resigned
to what he must accept
and as he settles
he loses something
that fish by definition must have

Sunset in My Eyes

Driving cross-country
smoking cheap cigars
there is only one way
to go home, despite
many roads I've taken.
For some reason, I
can't explain, ZZ Top
never goes out of style
and the yucca lining
the ditch, a red-wing
on a fence post, bugs
dead on the windshield,
sunset in my eyes—all
speak the same place.

The Anchor

Look inward, there is a field
inside you full of daisies
and clover, honeybees
and all the things to make a soul.

All around you is dying gas—
a suffocating mirror
an unfulfilled guest
frustrated lust

but deep within the field
at sunrise, or in midnight
the breeze stirs, pollen floats
and you know there is more

to life than cubicles and charts,
keyboards and media bombs.
You know the anchor is rusting;
soon you will break free.

A Dim Glow

In American darkness
rain tapping on a country roof
the cold falls to winter,
a puppy stranded outside

scratches the door
hoping to return inside
but the dark within
is like the dark without.

The season closes
and the chill is what happens
when we fail to cover
our bets, when dying

leaves are ignored—
the wet bark of enduring limbs
countered only by a dim glow
of leftover promise.

Forgotten

Just about all
we want is to be
remembered

more than mere cedar
on a nameless prairie.

A mowing machine
works nearby

the smell of death
cuts a swath
through memory

blades of conformity.

About the Author

When not teaching or traveling around the country giving readings, Ken Hada lives on a plot of ground northwest of Ada, Oklahoma. His poetry has received The Wrangler Award from the National Western Heritage Museum. He has twice been a finalist for the Oklahoma Book Award, a finalist for the Spur Award and has been featured on The Writer's Almanac. Contact information and other details available at www.kenhada.org

ACKNOWLEDGMENTS

With gratitude to the editors of the journals and anthologies where the following poems first appeared:

Aint Nobody that can Sing Like Me: "The Hard luck of Dying Young" & "Train" & "Leveling" & "Zen and the Sensitive Redneck"
Blood & Thunder: "At Forty-Six"
Blue Hole: "Blue" & "Glistening Longhorns"
California Quarterly: "The Anchor"
Concho River Review: "When O'Keeffe Found a Skull" & "Texas Rain"
Dragon Poet Review: "Young Mother on a Train" & "Roots" & "Blue River Lion" & "Sunset in My Eyes" & "Abiding" & "Winter"
Elegant Rage: A Poetic Tribute to Woody Guthrie: "Great Grandpa Gustava" & "Tire Swing" & "A Road"
I-70 Review: "Whippoorwill"
Illya's Honey: "Old Man Henry" & "A Bell" & "Worship Hour" & "Texas Swing" & "Silverton, Texas"
Licking River Review: "Rituals at Dusk"
Like Father, Like Sun CD: "A Road" & "Jazz" & "Great Grandpa Gustava" & "A Dim Glow"
Neustadtfestival.com: "Our Lady of Guadalupe Church: Navajo Dam"
Oklahoma Today: "Fallen"
Our New Orleans: "Jouissance (New Orleans)" & "Raindrops on a Plastic Coffee Lid" & "On the Corner: Royal & St. Ann"
Poetrybay: "In Darkness" & "When I was a Heron" & "Hunger"
Red River Review: "The Poets' Lament" & "How it All Started" & "Disquieting" & "Forgotten" & "When I Dream" & "Mystery" & "Arcing" & "A Few Days After the Funeral" & "Yellow School Bus" & "Flapping in Wind" & "Death on a River" & "Bear Dreams" & "Expectations" & "Settling"
San Pedro River Review: "Prescilianos Café" & "San Juan Relief" & "In My Father's House" & "Of Men & Machinery" & "Dusk" & "Janitor" & "Coffee Cycle" & "Pastoral: Near McAlester, Oklahoma"
Silentspringat50.org: "A Savior Dressed in Yellow"
Sugarmule.com: "Flagman on a Road Crew" & "Morning Chore" & "East of Austin" & "The Hard Luck of Not Dying Young" &

"Train" & "Leveling" & "Zen and the Sensitive Redneck"
Swtxpca.org: "Chanson d'adventure: New Mexico Railrunner Express"
The Enigmatist: "A Night like This"
This Land: "Homecoming" & "Going Home" & "For This Time, at Least"
Travelin Music: a Poetic Tribute to Woody Guthrie: "Bring an Extry Mule"
Voices de le Luna: "A Night like This" & "White River Repose"
Whale Road Review: "Night Sounds"

"Homecoming" was one of two finalists for the Spur Award from Western Writers of America, 2015

"Forgotten" was nominated for a 2015 Pushcart Prize.